Paul Davenport

Buried Treasure on Indian Island

DELTA Publishing

You can listen to *Buried Treasure on Indian Island* using the free DELTA Augmented app – you'll also find fun interactive activities!

Download the free DELTA Augmented app onto your device | Start picture recognition and scan the **contents page** | Download files and use them now or save them for later

Photos:
4 Shutterstock (Nomad_Soul), New York; **5** Shutterstock (mckenna71), New York; **9, 54** Getty Images (goodvector), München; **84** Shutterstock (Ka Han), New York; **91** Shutterstock (Martial Red), New York; **92** Shutterstock (Kheng Guan Toh), New York; **93** Shutterstock (Romie Miller), New York; **93** Shutterstock (Zigi_rs), New York

1st edition 1 5 4 3 2 1 | 2025 24 23 22 21

Delta Publishing, 2021
www.deltapublishing.co.uk

Text: Paul Davenport
Annotations and activities: Bernardo Morales
Editor: Kate Baade
Illustrations and Cover picture: Grit Döhnel
Design: Datagroup int, Timisoara
Cover picture: Grit Döhnel
Printing and binding: Salzland Druck GmbH, Staßfurt

ISBN 978-3-12-501144-1

Contents

Abbreviations

sth = something
sb = somebody
inf =informal

Before you start

1. What is a "Native American"? How did they live in the past? And today? Use the internet to help you complete the table.

Native American	
In the past	Today
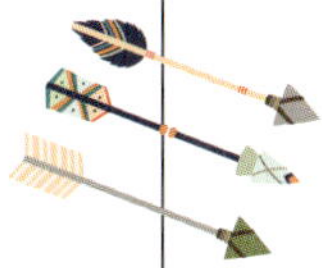 	

2. Around 30% of Native Americans live on reservations. What are reservations? What is life like on reservations?

3. One of the characters in the story has Native American roots. When Native Americans die, their bodies go to a burial ground. Why do you think Len feels uncomfortable about going to a burial ground?

4. Read the story. Were you right?

Chapter 1

It was the sixteenth of July, three weeks into the summer vacation, a good day for 11-year-old Tim Nolan and his friends, all of them sixth graders at Madawaska Middle School. They were excited. They had started a club, the Sunset Club, as they called it, and were busy building a clubhouse. Every morning, the four of them, Pete, Len, Carter and Tim met and rode to the woods at the edge of town. There they hid their bikes and continued on foot. The clubhouse was located near the shore of Long Lake and about a ten-minute walk from where they entered the woods.

Today, after three weeks of hard work, they finished the clubhouse. They were tired but happy. It was time for a little celebration! One of them had to go for pizza and soft drinks. They drew lots. Pete was the 'lucky' one. The others decided to make a sign while waiting. They sawed off a piece of a leftover board and wrote in large letters the words THE SUNSET CLUB on it. Then they nailed it over the door and stood back to admire their work.

When Pete returned shortly after, they went inside and dug into the pizzas. For the next several minutes, no one said anything. They were too busy eating. Except for Carter. As usual, he had one eye on his Smartphone. Suddenly, he looked up and said, 'Storm warning! A big storm with high winds is heading our way. It's in the Portland area and moving fast.'

'We finished the clubhouse just in time!' Pete said.

Tim knocked on the wall and looked around at the others. 'Yeah, but did we build it strong enough? Will it still be standing after the storm?'

That night the storm hit Madawaska and lasted until nine the next morning. When Tim got up and looked out his bedroom

---

5 **clubhouse** a building where people can meet – 7 **on foot** walking – 8 **shore** the area of land that separates land and water – 13 **to draw lots** when you draw lots you choose who will do sth by taking a piece of paper from a bowl or container – 14 **to saw sth off** to cut sth with a saw, tool for cutting wood – 14 **leftover** part of sth that hasn't been used – 15 **board** a flat piece of wood – 16 **to admire** to look at sth that is attractive – 18 **shortly** soon – 19 **several** a small number, usually three or four

window, he couldn't believe his eyes. There were broken branches everywhere. The yard was covered with branches, the driveway, too. But the biggest shock of all was what he saw when he looked behind the house. There, in the middle of the garden, lay the Nolans' beloved apple tree. Sometime in the night, the winds had knocked it over!

His first thought was the clubhouse. *Is it still there? Or has it been blown apart?* He closed his eyes and took a deep breath. *Three weeks of hard work - all for nothing?*

He ate breakfast quickly, jumped on his bike and headed for the woods. When he got there, he hid his bike in the usual place and went on by foot. It wasn't easy going. Fallen trees blocked his path. He had to walk around them or climb over them. As he neared the clubhouse, he grew more and more nervous. A little further now and he would see it, or what was left of it. He held his breath.

'Phew!' There it was! Tim let out a loud laugh. *Thank goodness, it's still standing!* he said to himself. Then he went up closer and looked at it from all sides. Except for a small hole in the roof and a cracked window, there were no further signs of damage. He opened the door and looked inside. The comic books and the cards were still on the table, even the empty soft drink cans were still in place. He nodded and smiled to himself. *We did a good job! The clubhouse is storm proof! Great work, guys!*

When he went outside again and looked around, he began to realize how powerful the storm had been. The strong winds had pushed over some very large trees. In fact, one of the largest had fallen very close to the clubhouse. *A few feet to the right and...* Tim squeezed his eyes shut and pictured what had almost happened.

---

1 **branch** the part of a tree where flowers and leaves grow – 2 **driveway** a private road that connects to the main road – 8 **to blow apart** to destroy – 11 **woods** forest – 13 **path** a route in the forest where you can walk – 20 **cracked** damaged with think lines, but not completely broken – 23 **to nod** to move your head up and down to show you are happy or agree with sb – 24 **proof** protected against sth – 29 **to squeeze your eyes shut** to close your eyes

On his way out of the woods, he was still thinking about the fallen trees when he had an idea. He stopped and smiled. Suddenly, his head was full of pictures. It was like he was watching a film, a video of him and his friends building a raft and riding it on the lake. *We can use those trees to build a raft! Yeah, we can build a raft and go riding on the lake! Maybe to Indian Island and back!* He let out a happy laugh, took out his Smartphone and sent the following message to Carter, Pete and Len:

Meet me at the clubhouse at noon.
Important!

He was so excited that he was smiling from ear to ear as he put the phone back in his pocket. But a moment later the smile vanished and he grew nervous. He could only think of one thing. How would his friends react to his idea? *Will they like it? Will they want to build a raft and go to Indian Island with me?*

Think about it...

Have you ever been in a club?

Why did you join?

4 **raft** a type of floating flat boat typically made out of pieces of wood tied together –
14 **to smile from ear to ear** to give a big smile

Chapter 2

When Tim got to the clubhouse it was shortly before twelve o'clock and no one was there. Nervous, he watched and waited for the others. A few minutes later, Carter showed up, then Pete, and finally, Len.

Tim watched as his three friends inspected the outside of the clubhouse and looked for signs of damage caused by the storm. Moments later, Len opened the clubhouse door and looked in. 'Hey! Everything's okay,' he said with a bright smile.

'Duh.' Pete rolled his eyes. 'What did you expect? We built it, didn't we?'

Carter took a deep breath and let it out slowly. 'But we were lucky.' He pointed at the huge tree that had fallen only a few

23 **to show up** to arrive – 31 **to take a deep breath** to breathe in deeply to help with relaxation

feet away. 'That tree could have flattened the clubhouse like a pancake!'

Tim nodded slowly. Then he smiled and said, 'When I came here early this morning to check on things, I was nervous, afraid that the storm had ruined our clubhouse. You can imagine how happy I was to see that it was still standing. But my mood changed when I saw all the knocked-down trees. At first, I felt kind of sad, but then I had an idea.'

'So that's what's so important,' Carter said with a little grin on his face. 'You had an idea. That's why we had to come here?' He looked around at the others and grinned some more, then turned back to Tim. 'Okay, we're listening,' he said in a flat voice, 'Your idea better be good.'

'It is good!' Tim said with a bright smile. He looked into the faces of his friends, then turned and pointed at the fallen trees. 'You see these trees? We can use them to build a raft and ride around the lake on it. Or we could even raft down to the end of the lake, maybe to Indian Island! What do you think of that?' he said.

'I'm for it,' said Pete immediately. 'I've always wanted to ride a raft. And I've always wanted to have a look around Indian Island,' he added.

Len said nothing. There was a worried look on his face.

Pete and Tim laughed. They were excited. Carter didn't laugh. He didn't get excited easily. First he asked questions, lots of questions. That was his way. If he got good answers to his questions, he might get excited. A little. After cleaning his glasses, he looked a long moment at the fallen trees, and then at Tim. 'What do you know about building a raft?'

'Hey, man, anyone can build a raft.' Tim looked at the others and rolled his eyes.

---

1 **to flatten** to crash on top of sth and make it flat – 6 **mood** the way you feel, e.g. happy, sad, etc. – 9 **grin** a naughty smile – 20 **to be for sth** to support an idea – 31 **to roll your eyes** to move your eyes in a way that shows sb has said sth silly or strange

Carter shook his head. 'I mean a *safe* raft, one that will carry the four of us.'

'Aw, come on, man. We can build a super safe raft,' Tim said.

'Yeah, don't be such a spoil sport, man!' Pete gave Carter a hard look.

'I'm not a spoil sport, but I'm not careless, either. This *is* serious business. We can't just go off on a rafting trip without making the necessary preparations.'

Tim nodded, a thoughtful look on his face. 'No question about it,' he said. 'This is serious business. You're right, of course. The raft has to be safe. I'll have a look in the Internet. I'm sure I can find something there.'

'Right. That would be the first step. But what do we know about rafting? Carter looked around at Pete and Len. 'Have either of you ever been on a raft?'

They shook their heads.

Carter turned back to Tim. 'What about you?'

'Uh, no, not really.' He forced a smile. 'But I've seen it done in the movies.'

'Oh, right. In the movies,' Carter said sarcastically.

Tim turned red.

'There's one more thing.' Carter paused a moment, to make sure everyone was paying attention. He pointed at a bird flying overhead. 'See that bird? It's free, isn't it, free to fly wherever it wants. You know the old saying, "Free as a bird".' He shook his head. 'But we're not so free, are we? We can't do anything we want. We sometimes have to ask our parents, don't we?'

Tim, Pete and Len all nodded.

'So what would our parents say if we asked them if we could build a raft and ride down the lake to the island?'

Nobody spoke.

'Well? What would they say? Would they let us do it or not?'

---

1 **safe** secure – 6 **spoil sport** sb whose behavior spoils everyone's fun – 6 **careless** sb who doesn't care about small details – 16 **to shake your head** to say no by moving your head – 20 **sarcastic** with irony

Tim hesitated. 'Of course they wouldn't. I, uh, thought maybe we could do it without telling them.'

Carter shook his head. 'That wouldn't work. They'd find out – sooner or later they'd find out.'

For a moment, Tim just looked at Carter. Finally he nodded.

Carter smiled. 'What we need is a dad to come with us. The question is, which dad? Mine's too busy.' He looked around at the others. 'What about yours?'

Len shook his head. 'My dad is not the outdoor type.'

'My dad has a bad back. He's got to have an operation,' Pete said.

They all looked at Tim. He was smiling. 'My dad *is* the outdoor type,' he said. 'I can ask him. I think he'll come with us.'

'Great!' said Pete and gave Tim the thumbs-up sign. 'Mr. Nolan is a cool guy. I like him.'

'Hey! This is going to be fun!' Tim let out a loud laugh and began giving fist bumps all around. When he got to Len, he stopped. 'What's the matter with you, man? Is something wrong?'

Len put his hands in his pockets and lowered his eyes.

'Uh, Len? You got a problem?'

Len hesitated some more but finally looked up and said, 'As you know, my grandma was a full-blooded Maliseet Indian. Before she died, she taught me a lot about how Indians think. One of the things she taught me about was Indian burial grounds. She said they are sacred places, places that connect Indians to their past, and the dead there must not be disturbed.' He paused a moment and then added, 'You've probably heard the stories in town. You know, the ones about the burial ground on the island.'

Tim gave a quick nod. 'Sure, we know about the stories.'

'Some strange things have happened there,' Len said nervously.

---

1 **to hesitate** to pause because you don't know what to say or because you are nervous – 3 **to find out** to catch sb doing sth – 9 **outdoor type** sb who enjoys outdoor activities – 13 **to give sb the thumbs-up** to put your hand in a position to show that you like sth – 16 **to give fist bumps** to put your fists against sb else's fist to show you agree – 21 **full-blooded** when both parents belong to the same race – 23 **burial ground** a place reserved to bury human bodies – 25 **to disturb** to move, to bother

Carter rolled his eyes and smiled. 'Hey, come on! They're just stories, man. There's nothing true about them.'

Len shook his head and gave Carter a dark look.

'Come on, buddy. You don't believe that stuff, do you?' Pete laughed.

'I do. Don't you?'

Taken by surprise, Pete grinned nervously. 'Hey, man, dead is dead. I don't believe the stories about bad things happening when you disturb Indian burial grounds. No way! You know what I think? I think the real reason you don't want to go there is because you're afraid.'

There was a moment of shocked silence. Len looked like he was about to explode. Tim turned to him and said, 'Don't pay any attention to Pete!' He put his arm around the boy's shoulder and smiled. 'It's alright. We can understand that you're worried. We don't think you should be, but we know that you are part Indian and we respect that, don't we, Pete?' For a moment, Pete said nothing. When he finally nodded, Tim turned again to Len and smiled. 'Indian Island is a large island. There's enough to see without going to the burial ground. If we do stumble on it, we'll just have a quick look, and then move on. Is that alright?' Len looked around. Pete had turned away, but Carter and Tim were smiling at him. Len hesitated, but finally smiled, too. 'Yeah, I guess so,' he said softly, but the worried look was still in his eyes.

Think about it...

- Why do you think Len was worried?
- Would you want to build a raft with your friends?

---

4 **buddy** friend – 9 **No way!** Not at all. – 20 **to stumble on sth** to find sth by chance

Chapter 3

That evening Tim gave out the good news that his father would go with them. Filled with excitement, the boys could hardly wait to start working on the raft the next day.

They met at the clubhouse the next morning at nine o' clock. Carter was in charge and gave them instructions for the day. He was the 'construction manager', the one who explained how to build the raft.

It was a lot of work but it was fun, too. Of course, there were some problems, mostly to do with Pete, who enjoyed teasing Len about his 'fear' of Indian burial grounds. But all in all, there was a good feeling in the air. They joked and laughed a lot. Building the

22 **can hardly wait** to be very excited about starting sth – 29 **to tease** to make fun of sb – 30 **all in all** generally

raft brought them closer together than ever before. They became a real team.

On a Monday afternoon, almost a week after they had started their work on the raft, they finished it. To celebrate the occasion, Tim handed out cans of cola and raised his in a toast. 'To our raft!' he said playfully. 'May it carry us to the island and back safely.'

'To our raft!' The others raised their cans and echoed him.

For several moments, they stood drinking their cola and looking at the raft silently.

'And now,' said Tim after a while, 'the moment of truth has come. It's time to test the raft to see how good it is.' He smiled. 'Come on, guys, let's get it into the water.'

They had built the raft on the shore of the lake, only a few feet from the water, but it was heavy, heavier than the boys thought it would be. For the next several minutes, they pulled and pulled, but the raft hardly moved. Finally, Carter raised his hand. 'Whoa! Stop! There's a better way to do this,' he said and pointed to a large branch that had broken off a tree in the storm.

The others looked to where he was pointing and nodded.

'So what we'll do is lift the front end of the raft a little, just enough to shove the branch under it. Then we're going to push the raft so that it slides over the branch.

'And you, Tim. You're our guy with the big muscles. You'll pull on the raft with the rope, okay?'

'That sounds like a plan,' Tim said with a grin.

And it was. On the third or fourth try, the raft began sliding over the branch. Tim got out of the way quickly. The boys pushed some more, then watched as the raft slid slowly into the water. The next moment, they let out a loud cheer. The raft was floating!

'It passed the test!' Pete cried.

---

11 **the moment of truth** the time when sth is tested – 17 **hardly** only a little – 21 **to lift** to raise sth, in this case, in order to move it – 22 **to shove** to push sth forward – 25 **rope** a long piece of thick string – 27 **to slide** to move smoothly over a surface, – 30 **to float** to stay on the surface and not go under water

Tim shook his head. 'Not yet, dude. When we're all on it and it's still floating, then it's passed the test!'

One by one, they climbed onto the raft, carefully, step by step. When they were all aboard, Tim laughed and said, 'Anyone got wet feet?'

The others all shook their head. Tim turned to Carter. 'No wet feet thanks to Carter! He's da man. He's the one who showed us how to build a raft and build it right! Good work, dude!' Tim gave him a high five and the others did the same.

Carter let out a laugh but a moment later he was serious again. 'There's one more thing: paddling! You've got to learn how to paddle before we go anywhere on that raft!' He looked at Tim. 'You haven't forgotten what we said about practicing paddling, have you?'

Tim let out a nervous laugh. 'Of course not! We've got to practice before we raft down the lake, I know that. We want to have a fun trip, but we want it to be safe, too.

I hid the paddles in the clubhouse. I'll be right back!'

Tim hurried off while the others stood around and waited. A few minutes later, he was back with the paddles under his arm. He gave each of the boys a paddle, then turned to Carter. 'It's your show, man. We're all ears.'

'Okay, let's get started,' Carter said. He first turned to Len. 'You and Tim go to the front, you on the right side, Tim on the left.' Then he nodded to Pete. 'You and I will be at the back, you on the right side, me on the left.'

'What about Mr. Nolan?' Len wanted to know.

'He'll be in the middle,' said Carter.

As soon as they were all in position, Carter raised his arm and said, 'Okay. When I give the signal, dig your paddle down deep

---

7 **da man** (*inf*) an expression to show thanks and respect – 11 **to paddle** to move a boat using paddles / oars – 18 **paddle** long poles with flat ends used to move a boat – 21 **It's your show** (*inf*) expression to show that sb is in show – 22 **to be all ears** to be waiting to hear sth

and pull it through the water. Like this!' Carter raised his paddle, pushed it down into the water and pulled it. 'Got it?' he shouted.

'Got it!' the others said.

'Now it's your turn! Go for it!'

The boys started paddling and, very slowly at first, the raft started moving. After a while, as they continued to paddle, it picked up speed, little by little. Moments later, Tim let out a joyful cry and the others echoed him. It was a wonderful feeling! They were riding on their own raft, the raft they had built themselves!

Back on shore, that good feeling was still with them. Their eyes were shining with pride! Their raft had passed the test - and they had passed the test, too! But tomorrow was the real thing. Tomorrow they would raft to the island! Tim looked around at the others. They were just as excited as he was!

Think about it...

How does working on something with your friends make you feel?

When was the last time you were proud of something you did?

7 **joyful** happy, full of joy – 11 **pride** the satisfaction you feel when you've done sth good

Chapter 4

That night Tim found it difficult to get to sleep. He was worried about what might happen on the trip. When he finally fell asleep, he had a bad dream. It was about a ship that hit a rock and sank. He was the captain. It was his mistake. As the ship was going down, the crew was pointing their fingers at him and shouting. His pounding heart woke him up. He felt terrible. He was wide awake now, his eyes wide open. The dream wouldn't go away. At last, after what seemed like hours, he fell asleep again.

But early the next morning, when he and his father rode to the woods to meet the others, he was so excited that he forgot all about his worries. The sun was just coming up when they reached the clubhouse. They went inside, got the paddles and hurried down to the lake. The raft was there, right where they had left it.

There was still fog on the lake, but it was lifting fast. There was little or no wind, perfect weather for rafting. Tim looked down the lake. As usual, it was empty, not a boat was in sight. A few

23 **pounding heart** when your heart beats fast because you're nervous

years ago, that had been different. Back then, the water was clean and there were lots of things to do on the lake. There was boating, fishing, swimming, or just relaxing. Back then, Long Lake had been a popular place.

But now the lake was as empty as a ghost town. There had been an 'accident' at the Madawaska Paper Mill. A large quantity of toxic water from the mill had flowed into the river that ran into the lake. It had killed all the fish and almost killed the lake, too! The lake had changed. It looked different. It smelled different. It was different! At the public landing there was a large sign: WARNING! THIS WATER IS POLLUTED. SWIM AT YOUR OWN RISK!

Tim's father climbed onto the raft first. Carter, Pete and Len followed him. Tim untied the rope and got on last. He looked around. His dad smiled and gave him a thumbs-up sign. It was a magic moment! They were pumped up and ready to go. Tim gave a signal and they all began to paddle. Indian Island was about three miles down the lake. If all went well, they would be there in less than an hour.

A short time later, a light wind came up, but the raft was moving along smoothly and everyone was in a good mood. There was lots of loud joking and laughing. Normally, the boys would be busy with their Smartphones, but they had agreed not to use them until they reached the island. As Carter said, you can't paddle with a Smartphone in your hand! They missed their phones, but now they were actually talking with each other and that felt good, too.

After a while, the wind grew stronger and began blowing directly in their faces. The boys had to paddle harder. When Carter complained about the wind and the waves, Tim turned to Len and said, 'What do you say, man? Have you got a little song

---

7 **toxic** poisonous, dirty – 7 **mill** a factory where things are produced – 11 **polluted** dirty – 14 **to untie** to undo a knot – 16 **to be pumped up** to be excited and full of energy – 30 **wave** when the sea is not calm there are waves

for us? You know? Something with a good beat, one that will help us paddle against the wind?'

Len looked at him as if he had said something strange. 'A song?'

'Yeah, a song! Don't be modest. We all know how good you are at rapping!'

Len gave him that look again.

'Come on, man. Give us a break!'

'Yeah, Len, I'd love to hear you rap,' Mr. Nolan said with a laugh.

'Okay, one song,' said Len and smiled. 'But you've all got to join in.'

Tim looked around at the others, and then turned back to Len. 'No problem,' he said. 'We're with you!'

Len thought for a moment. 'Okay. You all know the old sea shanty "What shall we do with a drunken sailor?"'

'Sure we do,' Tim said.

Len let out a little laugh. 'Well, I'm going to do a rap version of it. As soon as I finish, we'll do it together.' He created a beat by snapping his fingers. Then he began to rap. On his signal, the others joined in.

After the first verse and the refrain, Len suddenly fell silent.

Tim looked at him, but Len didn't react. 'Hey, you're not finished already, are you? We just got started.'

'Sorry, I can't remember how it goes from there.'

'Hey, come on! You're a rapper! You can make up the rest! Don't let us down now, man!'

Len had to smile. He liked the attention he was getting. 'Just a sec, I'll think of something. Okay, here goes: Put him on a diet of bread and water, put him on a diet of bread and water, put him on a diet of bread and water, early in the morning.'

He nodded his head and the others repeated the verse.

Len hesitated a moment, then nodded. 'Next verse. Rap after me! Put him in jail and throw away the key, put him in jail and

---

4 **modest** not talking about or showing off your abilities – 12 **sea shanty** a type of song sung by sailors when working together – 16 **beat** a rhythm that repeats regularly – 19 **refrain** a part of a song that is repeated – 23 **to make up** to create, to invent – 24 **to let sb down** to disappoint sb

throw away the key, put him in jail and throw away the key, early in the morning.'

On his signal, the others did their best to rap it like Len.

'Okay, I got one more verse. Ready? Tie him to the mast till he dries out, tie him to the mast till he dries out, tie him to the mast till he dries out, early in the morning.'

Len had just finished when Tim raised his hand. The wind had grown even stronger and the waves had begun splashing against the front of the raft. 'Wait a minute!' he cried. 'It's getting too rough! We've got to get out of here before it's too late!'

'Yeah, we've got to get close to shore where there's not so much wind, where the water's calmer,' Carter said.

'Carter's right!' Mr. Nolan shouted.

'Okay, we'll turn the raft around and head for shore, full speed ahead!' Tim cried.

For the next several minutes, the boys paddled as hard as they could. The waves were pounding the side of the raft now and getting everyone wet, but the boys didn't stop. At last, when they got close to shore and the waves had calmed down, Tim turned to the others. 'Is everybody okay?'

Carter looked at him a moment, and then let out a dry laugh. 'Fine. Just cold, wet and scared silly!'

Tim had to laugh, too. He was familiar with Carter's black humor.

'What about you, Dad?' Tim said.

'I'm okay, just a little wet,' his father said with a smile.

'We were lucky,' Tim said. 'We got out of there just in time. From now on, we'll stay near the shore.'

'Maybe we should have done that from the start,' Carter said in a sharp voice. He shook his head. 'Right now we've got to do something about our wet clothes. We can't go on like this.'

---

1 **to throw sth away** to not keep sth, to put it in the trash – 4 **mast** a tall post on a boat – 8 **to splash** when liquid falls and hits sth, it splashes – 10 **rough** not calm, when there is a lot of wind and strong waves. – 17 **to pound** to hit hard

Tim hesitated, but then noticed that the others were nodding. 'Uh, yeah, sure,' he said. 'We'll go ashore and build a fire and get dried out.'

As soon as they reached shore, they went up and down the beach and soon found enough dry wood for a fire.

Tim looked in his pockets. 'We need something to start the fire with. Anybody got a lighter?'

'Here you go,' his father said and handed him a book of matches.

'What about paper? Anybody got some paper on them?'

At first no one said anything. Pete looked around, and then said, 'I've got a comic book with me, but I - '

'Come on, Pete. Only a page or two, okay?' Tim cut in.

Pete hesitated. Finally, he pulled the comic book out of his backpack, but turned away from the others so they couldn't see it. He tore two pages from it and handed them to Tim.

Tim smiled. 'Thanks, man.' He lit a match and held the flame under the paper until it caught fire. Then he bent down and put the burning paper between some pieces of wood.

The others watched as the wood slowly caught fire. Within minutes, there was a bright fire. They stepped in close to get dry.

'Those waves were scary. They just kept getting higher and higher. I thought they would wash me right off the raft,' Pete said in a shaky voice.

'Me, too,' said Len. 'It was like panic on the Titanic!'

'Shouldn't you have seen the waves sooner?' Carter said and gave Tim a hard look.

'Damn it!' Tim took a deep breath. 'If there's one thing I can't stand, it's a Monday morning quarterback!' he said in a sharp voice. 'It's always easy to criticize afterward. If you knew what to do why didn't you say so beforehand?'

'You're the head of this expedition! It was your idea!' Carter's eyes flashed.

---

2 **to go ashore** to move in the direction of land – 7 **lighter** sth that makes fire – 17 **to bend down** to move your body down – 23 **shaky** in quick movements. – 28 **Monday morning quarterback** sb who criticizes sth after it has happened – 31 **expedition** trip

Tim's father was about to say something, but decided it was better to let the boys settle their differences between themselves.

Tim's face grew red. 'That doesn't mean that you've got to follow orders blindly! This isn't the army, damn it!'

Carter opened his mouth to say something, but let out a laugh instead.

Suddenly, Len pointed at something down the lake. 'Hey! See that?'

'It's a large boat!' said Tim. 'It's heading for the mainland at the end of the lake.'

Carter was staring at the boat. 'That's weird. It was on the island. What was it doing on the island?'

Tim thought for a moment. 'Maybe it was some people who wanted to look around there just like us.'

'Yeah, maybe tourists,' said Mr. Nolan.

Carter shook his head. 'I still say it's weird! You hardly see any boats on the lake nowadays.'

Pete had stopped listening. He was staring at the fire. Suddenly, he looked around. 'Did anyone think to bring marshmallows with them?' he asked.

The others laughed. 'Leave it to Pete to think of marshmallows at a time like this,' Tim said with a shake of his head.

Think about it ...

Do you think the raft is good enough to get them to Indian Island?

The night before the trip, Tim had a bad dream. When was the last time you had a bad dream? What was it about?

---

3 **to grow red** to gradually become red – 4 **to follow orders blindly** to do what sb says without questioning them – 11 **weird** strange – 17 **nowadays** currently

Chapter 5

After a while, when their clothes were dry, everyone felt better. They put out the fire and climbed onto the raft. On Tim's signal, the boys started paddling.

At first they were silent, but not for long. 'Hey, Len, you're part Indian, right?' Pete said in a fake friendly voice.

Len shook his head. 'Not that again!'

'Yeah, that again! I was wondering if any of your ancestors are buried on Indian Island?'

'Could be,' Len said in a flat voice. 'Why do you want to know?'

'Oh, it's nothing. I'm just curious,' Pete said with a sly smile. 'I just thought that if you've got ancestors there, you'd want to go there and have a look,' he said and his smile grew wider.

For a moment, Len said nothing. Finally, he turned around and gave Pete a hard look. 'No comment,' he said.

'What does that mean?'

'It means I'm not going to talk with you about this. I don't like your attitude.'

17 **to climb** to move or go up – 32 **attitude** the way you feel about sth

Pete's eyes opened wide in fake surprise. 'My attitude? What's wrong with my attitude?'

'You got no respect.'

'No respect! Hey, did you hear that, guys?' Pete laughed and looked around. But the others weren't laughing and Mr. Nolan was giving him a cold stare.

After a while, they came to a cove. For a long moment, Tim looked up and down, from one end to the other. 'You know what I miss?' His voice was soft and thoughtful. 'I miss the lake the way it was before the 'accident', when dad and I went fishing here. There were all kinds of wildlife here back then. The bushes along the shore were full of birds, there were ducks and geese all around, and lots of deer. Of course, to see a moose was the most exciting sight of all! Right here, in this cove, there was often a moose or two, right Dad?'

'Right!' his father said. 'Moose are such huge animals! Whenever we saw one, we stopped fishing and just watched it.' A smile crossed his face, but a moment later the smile turned sad. 'I miss the lake the way it was, too. It was such a beautiful place.'

'Yeah, but then they almost killed it and it'll be years before it comes back to life,' Carter said in an angry voice. 'Thanks a lot, Madawaska Paper Mill!'

'At least they had to pay a big fine, one million dollars to the town,' said Len.

Carter shook his head. 'Hah! That's peanuts to them. They should have paid a lot more!'

'See that 'for sale' sign?' Tim pointed to a camp in the cove. 'Almost every camp has one of those in its yard now. That's sad, really sad.'

'Yeah, and some people are buying camps cheap and waiting until the lake is clean again,' Carter said, 'so they can sell them for big money!'

---

7 **cove** a little bay – 11 **wildlife** animals that live outside – 16 **huge** very big – 25 **peanuts** (*here*) not a lot of money

Tim shook his head. 'Dirty lake, dirty money!' His voice was filled with anger.

For a moment, nobody spoke. Pete saw his chance. 'Hey, can we take a break? I got to have something to drink,' he said.

Tim let out a laugh. 'Can't it wait? We're not far from the island now.'

'Come on, man. Just five minutes.'

'Okay, five minutes for Pete to have his drink.' Tim looked at his watch and put down his paddle. When he turned around, Pete was digging into his backpack. He watched him a moment, and then said, 'What have you got there?'

'Uh, nothing.' Pete let out a nervous laugh. 'I was, uh, just checking to see if my phone got wet.'

Tim gave the others a knowing look. 'Uh huh,' he said and nodded slowly, as if he believed him.

'Does it still work?' Carter said, poker-faced.

Pete's face had turned red. 'Uh, yeah, as good as ever,' he said. He stuffed the phone into his backpack, pulled out a bottle and took a long drink.

A little later, Tim looked at his watch. 'Okay, we've had our five-minute break. It's time to be on our way again.' He looked at Len, then turned to the others. 'Everybody ready?'

'We're ready,' they all said at once.

'Wait a minute.' Tim turned to Len. 'How about another rap? It's easier to paddle when everyone's rapping!'

Len hesitated. 'Sorry, I don't feel like it right now,' he said finally.

Tim looked at him a moment and smiled. 'It's okay. It was just an idea.'

Pete laughed. 'What's the matter with Len?' he said in a sarcastic voice. 'Has he lost his voice?'

---

10 **to dig** to put your hand or a tool down into a deep place – 16 **poker-faced** not showing what your are really thinking or feeling

Tim turned around and looked Pete in the eye. 'You heard what he said. He doesn't feel like rapping right now!'

'Why not?' Pete shot back.

'That's Len's business. If he doesn't want to rap, he doesn't want to rap, that's all, so just accept it and let him be, okay?'

There was a big grin on Pete's face. 'I know why. He's too busy worrying about the burial ground.'

Carter gave Pete a sharp look. 'Let it go, man!'

Pete rolled his eyes and looked away.

For the next several minutes, no one spoke as the boys paddled along the shoreline. When they reached the end of the cove and came out the other side, they could see the island.

'Indian Island, straight ahead!' shouted Tim with a happy laugh.

Think about it...

What mistake do you think the boys made?
What would you do to get there faster?

Do you think Pete is being unkind to Len?
Why?

8 **to give sb a sharp look** to show sb that you aren't happy with them – 11 **shoreline** the line that divides water and land

Chapter 6

As they neared the island, everyone fell silent again. Tim was thinking about the bad feelings that had come up between him and Carter and between Pete and Len. He had begun to worry about the situation and hoped it would improve when they got to the island.

Mr. Nolan was thinking about Tim. He felt good about his son. He was proud of the way Tim stood his ground when Carter criticized him.

The others were staring at the island. From a distance, it had seemed beautiful, but now that they were closer to it and saw how deep and dark the woods were, they began to feel uneasy.

'Hah! Indian Island! People say it's a pretty place. It doesn't look so pretty to me!" Pete let out a nervous laugh.

Tim turned to him. 'Maybe when we get there and have a look around, you'll think differently. You know the old saying, "Don't judge a book by its cover".'

Pete wasn't sure what Tim meant, but he smiled and said, 'Before we look around we're going to eat, right? I'm starved,' he said and patted his stomach.

'That's Pete. Always thinking of the next meal,' Carter laughed.

'Maybe you should be, too,' Pete said in a sharp voice, 'a skinny guy like you!'

As soon as they were close enough to shore, Tim jumped into the water and pulled the raft behind him. On shore, he tied it to a tree and the others got out. They walked across the soft sand to a large, flat rock, climbed up on it and sat down. The sun was warm but the breeze from the lake was cool.

'The perfect place to have our lunch,' Pete said.

They ate quickly and then lay down on the warm rock with their backpacks under their heads. They closed their eyes and enjoyed the warmth of the sun on their skin. After a while, they got up and looked around.

---

7 **to stand your ground** to defend yourself – 11 **uneasy** insecure, not comfortable – 15 **Don't judge a book by its cover** you can't know how sth will be just by looking at the outside – 19 **to pat** to touch something again and again – 27 **breeze** light wind

'What do you want to do first? Any ideas?' Tim asked.

'Why don't we walk around the island?' Len said.

'That would be too hard,' Tim said. 'The shoreline is very rocky. Anyone got another idea?'

'We could explore the woods,' said Carter.

'And look for the burial ground!' Pete added.

'I knew you'd say that!' Len shook his head angrily at Pete.

'Listen, Len,' Tim said slowly. 'We know how you feel about the burial ground, but it would be okay just to have a look at it, wouldn't it? That wouldn't disturb the dead, would it?'

'Yeah,' Carter said, 'We'd just take a quick look at it and then be on our way. There's nothing wrong with that, is there?'

Len lowered his eyes. 'I- I don't know. I don't think it's right, but if you say so...'

'Good man,' said Tim, and put his arm around him. 'Everything's going to be alright, buddy. You can trust us!'

They put on their backpacks and headed for the woods.

Think about it...

The boys were feeling uneasy about how the woods looked. How would you feel?

Why do you think Len doesn't want to see the burial grounds?

Chapter 7

In a little hut in the middle of the island, two men were drinking coffee. George Haley and Johnny Hogan were guards. Not far from the hut was the Indian burial ground. Their job was to guard it.

Johnny slapped at his neck. 'These damned mosquitoes! I hate this island!' he said.

George rolled his eyes. 'Ever heard of mosquito spray?'

'You got some?'

'Yeah, but not for you,' George laughed. 'You'll have to buy your own.'

'Come on, man. Just a little.'

'Uh-uh, not even a little.'

Johnny gave him a cold look. 'Okay, I'll do it my way.' He took out some paper and tobacco and began rolling himself a cigarette. As soon as he finished, he lit it and blew several rings of smoke into the air, one after the other.

19 **hut** a small building – 21 **guard** sb who makes sure a place is secure

When the smoke began to fill the hut, George got up quickly and opened the window. 'Bah! Those strong cigarettes are going to kill you,' he said in an angry voice.

'That's better than giant mosquitoes biting me to death,' Johnny said with a wild laugh.

For a long moment, George stood by the window and looked out before sitting down again. 'It's a stupid job,' he said. 'We guard the burial ground, day after day, seven days a week, but nothing happens.'

Johnny blew another smoke ring. 'But some day something *could* happen. And then we've got to be ready! Besides, the pay is good. And with my big family, I need the money,' he laughed.

George took a long last drink of his coffee and got up again. This time he opened the door to let out more smoke. He stood there a moment and looked out. After a while he turned to Johnny and frowned. 'What do you think? How much longer will we be here? How long will it take to finish the job?'

'You know what Big Boss said: Two more months or so - till the end of September.'

George shook his head. 'I know what he said but I find it hard to believe. We've been here for almost two months already and how many graves have they dug up? They won't be finished by Christmas at the rate they're going!'

'Hey, what's your big hurry?' Johnny said and smiled. 'You know they have to dig slowly and carefully. Big Boss gets very angry when they break something. Things like jugs or pots are worth much less when they get broken. We're talking about big money here! Hah! There's buried treasure on Indian Island, man! Just one unbroken pot is worth up to twenty thousand dollars!'

George looked at him but said nothing.

'Besides, they have to fill in each grave when they finish with it to make everything look normal again.'

---

16 **to frown** to move your eyebrows down to show you're being serious – 29 **pot** container made by hand

'Okay, okay!' George said with a nervous smile. 'You're right but - ' He took in a deep breath.

'But what?'

'But a little action once in a while would be good. Just a little. Just enough to break the routine and keep us on our toes.'

Johnny thought for a moment, then shook his head. 'I don't think anyone will come here, but if they do - ' he laughed suddenly and patted his rifle - 'we've got these!'

'Hopefully, we won't need to use them. If someone does come here and see the grave robbers, we'll do what the boss told us to do. We'll tell them they're archeologists.'

'Do you think people will believe that?' Johnny asked.

'Probably not. That's why it's important to keep people away from the burial ground.'

'Right. That's our job, isn't it?'

George looked at his watch. 'Bob and Luis will be here soon. It's my turn to go and meet them.'

'Luis has got tobacco for me. Can you pick it up?'

'Sure, if you give me the money,' George said.

'I gave him the money already.'

'You trust Luis? What if he doesn't have the tobacco?'

Johnny shook his head. 'He wouldn't do that. He knows me better than that.'

George forced a smile and looked at his watch again. 'Well, I'd better go now. See you later.'

'Don't forget the tobacco.'

Think about it...

- Why do you think the burial grounds need a security guard?
- Why do you think they are taking so long to dig up the graves?

---

10 **grave robber** sb who steals things from graves

Chapter 8

Bob and Luis got into the boat and headed for the island. The boat moved silently through the water. It had an electric motor.

For a long moment, the men were silent, too, but then the small, dark-haired man suddenly laughed.

'What are you laughing about?' Bob said.

'I was just thinking. You were there when the boat from the island landed, weren't you?'

'Sure I was, and you were, too.'

Luis looked him in the eye and said, 'Have you ever asked yourself how much a boat full of that Indian stuff is worth?'

Bob thought a moment. 'Hard to say,' he said after a while. 'Maybe about $400,000.'

27 **to land** to arrive, usually used to talk about planes or boats – 30 **stuff** things

Luis nodded and said, 'That's a lot of money, man!'

'You're right about that!' Bob said with a laugh.

'Have you ever thought about what you could do with that much money?'

Bob suddenly stopped laughing. 'No, have you?'

There was a sly smile on Luis's face. 'The winters here in northern Maine are long and cold. Where I come from the sun shines all year long.'

Bob's eyes opened wide. 'So?'

'So I don't want to live here the rest of my life.'

Bob nodded his head slowly. 'I can understand that,' he said.

'With 200,000 dollars I could live where it's warm,' Luis said and smiled. 'I could buy me a beautiful house by the sea and a big boat and motor, and go fishing every day.'

'With 200,000 dollars?'

'Yeah, the other 200,000 would be for you.'

Bob's eyes grew wider.

'Listen, we could rent a van, pack the stuff in it and head for Boston. I know a guy there who will pay cash for the whole load. Then we split the money and go our separate ways.' Luis gave Bob a warm smile. 'Or you could come with me to Mexico. Life is good there when you've got money.'

For several moments, Bob said nothing. Then, suddenly, he started laughing. 'Nice plan, man, but it wouldn't work.'

'Why not?'

'Because Big Boss would find out and come after us.' Bob said with a shake of his head. 'We wouldn't get far.' He paused a moment, and then added, 'Besides, I'm from Maine. I like the weather here, the summer *and* the winter.'

'You're crazy. All you guys from Maine are crazy. No wonder they call you maniacs.'

---

6 **sly** in a way that shows that you have a clever plan or idea – 17 **to grow wider** to get bigger with surprise – 18 **van** a big vehicle that you can put a lot of things in – 20 **to split** to divide

Luis opened his mouth, as if to say more, then shook his head and fell silent.

A few moments later they reached the island and pulled the boat on shore. They took a quick look around, and then entered the woods.

Think about it ...

- If you were one of the guards, how would you feel?
- Why do you think Bob is nervous about Luis' plan?

Chapter 9

Tim led the way into the woods. He had to move slowly. The woods were thick and dark – and dangerous! They hadn't gone far when Carter fell and cut his hand on a rock. Then Len ran into a branch that almost poked his eye out. A few minutes later, Pete let out a frightened cry when he almost stepped on a snake. 'I've had it! Let's get out of here!' he shouted.

'Wait a minute!' Mr. Nolan held up his hand. 'Hey! Over there! Isn't that a path?'

Tim stopped and looked around. 'You're right!' he cried. 'Come on. Let's go for it!'

There was still a lot of woods between them and the path, but they moved more quickly now. The sight of the path had given them new energy.

When they finally got there, they began talking loud and laughing, so loud that Tim had to tell them to quiet down because the burial ground might be nearby.

'Yeah, yeah, for Len!' Pete hissed.

'It's not just for Len,' Tim said. 'It's for all of us. It's a matter of respect, respect for the dead.'

They had been walking several minutes, when Tim turned around and said, 'Do you see what I see? Up ahead.'

'Yeah, it's a sign,' Carter said.

'Come on,' Tim said. 'Let's check it out!'

They hurried along the path until they were standing in front of the sign. Tim took a step closer to it. 'It says MALISEET BURIAL GROUND - PLEASE RESPECT OUR DEAD BROTHERS AND SISTERS.'

'Cool!' Pete cried.

Tim noticed that Len had a strange look on his face. 'What's wrong, man?' he said.

---

4 **to poke** to push an object into sth – 5 **frightened** scared, afraid – 6 **I've had it!** I've had enough! – 16 **nearby** not too far away – 17 **to hiss** to say sth very quietly – 24 **to hurry** to walk more quickly so you can get somewhere faster

'Uh, you guys go ahead.' Len forced a smile. 'I'll wait for you here.'

Pete rolled his eyes. 'Did you hear that? Len has got cold feet. Cold, cold feet. Poor little Lenny.'

Len's face and neck turned a deep red. He opened his mouth as if to speak, but nothing came out.

Tim shook his head at Pete, then turned to Len. 'It's all right. Just ignore him. He's got a big mouth, that's all.'

Len nodded slowly.

'Wouldn't it be better if you stayed with us? Tim put his hand on Len's shoulder. 'All we're going to do is take a quick look at the place.'

For a long moment, Len looked Tim in the eye. Finally, he took in a deep breath and let it out slowly. 'Okay, I'm with you,' he said.

Tim smiled at him again, then turned to the others. 'Okay, let's go, but don't forget! We're near the burial ground now. Let's keep the volume down.'

They began walking faster now. Len tried to keep up with them but something was slowing him down. It was the way his grandmother had talked about Indian burial grounds. She had warned him that bad things could happen if he got too close to them. Her words echoed in his mind. It was as if she was right there beside him. A strange, dark feeling rose up inside him.

When they reached the burial ground and he saw all the graves, the feeling grew stronger. Suddenly, he realized that it was wrong for him to be there. He turned to Tim and said, 'I, uh, don't feel well. I think I've got to vomit.' He put his hand on his stomach. 'I'll be right back.'

Pete shook his head and let out a sarcastic laugh.

---

3 **to get cold feet** to become scared of sth at the last minute – 8 **to have a big mouth** to talk a lot, to say too much – 17 **to keep the volume down** to be quiet – 18 **to keep up** to walk at the same speed as other people – 24 **to reach** (*here*) to arrive

Tim nodded. 'Go ahead. We'll wait for you here.'

Len hurried up a little hill beside the burial ground and didn't stop until he had reached the top. When he got there, he leaned against a tree. The dark feeling, like a shadow, had followed him, stronger than before. He was dizzy now. He closed his eyes and took several deep breaths. Finally, the feeling left him and he opened his eyes again. He looked down the hill where the others were. Suddenly, he saw someone come up from behind them. *'Oh, my God! He's got a gun!'* he whispered and ducked behind the tree.

Think about it ...

Why do you think the boys are keeping the volume down?

Do you think it was a good idea to enter the burial ground?

5 **dizzy** a feeling that everything around you is moving in circles – 9 **to duck** to move the upper part of your body down very quickly

Chapter 10

'Hi, guys. What's up?'

When Tim and the others turned around, they were facing a big man with a smile on his face and a rifle in his hand. He was looking at Mr. Nolan.

'Oh, Hello. This is my son' - Mr. Nolan nodded at Tim - 'and his friends. We, uh, just wanted to have a look at the burial ground,' he said in a nervous voice.

'That's unusual. Most people are afraid to come here.'

27 **rifle** a gun

Mr. Nolan let out a little laugh. 'Afraid? We're not afraid, just interested, that's all.'

'How did you get here?' the man asked.

'On a raft. The boys built a raft and we rode it down the lake,' Mr. Nolan said with a proud smile.

The man shook his head, as if he couldn't believe his ears. He looked at the boys. 'You built a raft yourselves! Hey! I like that!' he laughed. 'I did that, too, when I was your age. Well, if you would like to see the burial ground, I can show you around. It's, uh, part of my job. My job is to guard the burial ground.'

Carter raised his eyebrows in surprise. 'Guard the burial ground? But why?'

The man made a worried face. 'Not everyone who comes here has the right attitude. Some come to make trouble. They want to make a lot of noise and see if the so-called spirits will react. They have no respect for the dead.'

Tim was about to ask him another question when the man's cell phone rang. He turned away from the boys and began talking. The call didn't last long. It was Bob. He was angry. He and Luis had started working ten minutes ago. *Where are you?* When the call ended he turned back to the boys and forced a smile. 'That was, uh, my buddy, the other guard. He says he needs my help. I've got to go, but first I'm going to give you guys that guided tour I promised. Are you ready?'

'Ready!' Tim said quickly.

The tour was short. The man seemed nervous. After less than ten minutes, he smiled, said goodbye and wished Mr. Nolan and the boys good luck on their trip back. He stood and watched them as they went back down the path they came from. Then he turned quickly and went off in the opposite direction.

11 **to raise your eyebrows** to move your eyebrows upwards – 14 **to make trouble** to create problems – 15 **to make noise** to be loud

When they had walked a little while, Tim looked around and saw that the man was no longer there. He looked at his father and shook his head. 'What was that all about?' he said.

'I don't know,' said his father. 'But I do know that he was lying.'

Tim nodded. 'Did you notice that he only showed us this side of the burial ground? He didn't want to take us around to the other side, did he?'

'Strange,' Carter said with a shake of his head, 'very strange!'

Think about it...

- Do you think the boys will get into trouble at the burial ground?
- What did Carter think was strange? Do you agree?

2 **no longer** not anymore

Chapter 11

Where is Len? Tim said to himself as he and the others looked down the path towards the place where he had climbed the hill. They thought he would come down any moment. But he didn't. They waited for what seemed like several minutes. 'Where can he be?' Tim said after a while. He gave the others a worried look. 'Something's wrong! We've got to look for him!'

Pete laughed. 'He's such a wimp. He probably ran off in panic when he saw the man with the rifle.'

Carter shook his head at Pete and said, 'That's not like Len and you know it! Maybe he's just having a little fun. Maybe he's waiting for us to come and look for him. When we do, he'll jump out from behind a tree or something and have a big laugh on us.'

'No way!' Tim said. 'This is the burial ground! He wouldn't do anything like that here!'

His father nodded. 'Tim's right! There's definitely something wrong. We'd better go look for him.'

As they went back down the path, Pete shouted out Len's name.

Tim put his fingers to his lips. 'Hey! Not so loud! Len wouldn't want that!'

When they got to the place where Len went up the hill, they spread out and began looking. For the next several minutes, they searched the whole area, but Len was not there.

They were really worried now. Tim looked around at the others. 'What do you think? What should we do?'

Carter was the first to speak. 'I think we should phone him.'

'Maybe it would be better to text him,' Tim said and gave Carter a knowing look. 'You know, in case there are others around.'

Carter's eyes opened wide. 'Do you think he's in danger?'

'I hope not. But if he is, he may need help.' Tim took out his Smartphone and wrote a message.

---

4 **to seem** to feel like – 7 **wimp** (*offensive*)sb who is easily scared – 7 **to run off** to escape – 22 **to spread out** to go in different directions

Where R U???

They all stared at the display screen of Tim's phone as they waited for Len's answer. But there was no answer. Finally, Tim typed another message.

Pls answer. Pls!

Again they waited, all eyes on the display screen. A long minute ticked by. Still no answer. Nothing!

Suddenly, they heard loud cries. Whoever it was, they were not far away and coming closer! Tim's heart began to pound. His eyes scanned the woods.

They all saw him at once. It was Len. He came crashing through the thick brush. His face was twisted in fear. 'Run!' he cried as soon as he saw them. 'They're after me!'

Tim reacted immediately. 'Run for the raft!' he shouted and started racing down the hill, the others close behind him.

Think about it ...

Why do you think the guard only shows them one side of the burial ground?

Why do you think Len didn't answer the text message?

4 **to stare** to look directly at something for a long time. – 14 **to scan** to look quickly and carefully at sth – 17 **to be after sb** to be chasing sb

Chapter 12

Tim's mind was racing as fast as his feet. *Who are 'they'? Why are they chasing Len? What are they doing on the island?* The answers to his questions, he realized, would have to wait. The important thing right now was to keep running.

After coming to the end of the path, they entered the woods. That slowed them down. They had to duck under branches and climb over logs now. But they pushed on until they finally caught sight of the lake. When they reached the shore, they jumped on the raft, pushed off and began to paddle.

Tim turned to Len. 'What's going on, man?' he said. 'Who's chasing you and why?'

'Two men - ' Len said in a breathless voice - 'I saw them from the top of the hill - on the other side of the burial ground - two men with shovels!'

'Shovels? What were they doing with shovels?'

'That's what I wanted to know,' Len said. 'That's why I watched them.'

'I don't believe this! Weren't you afraid?' Pete's mouth fell open.

'Sure I was - I was scared stiff but I *had* to find out what they were doing!'

'And then? What did you see?' Carter said quickly.

1 **to race** to go fast – 7 **log** large piece of wood – 7 **to catch sight of sth** to suddenly see sth – 14 **shovel** a tool you can use to dig holes in the ground – 20 **to be scared stiff** to be so afraid that you can't move

'They were digging - digging up graves! And filling sacks with the stuff they found!' Len said in a shaky voice.

'What did you do?' Tim said.

Len took a deep

breath and began slowly. 'At first I was shocked, but then I got angry. I had to get closer. I got down low and moved slowly down the hill. When I was close enough to see them clearly, I took out my phone and started taking photos.'

'And they saw you!' Mr. Nolan said.

'Yeah. One of them saw me and yelled at me. Then they started chasing me.'

'And you ran!' Pete said.

'For my life!' Len nodded quickly. His eyes were still wide with fear.

'We heard them!' Pete said. 'They were shouting at you to stop!'

'Yeah, they want those photos!'

'We can't let them get them!' Tim cried.

Mr. Nolan took out his Smartphone. 'You guys keep paddling, I'm going to call the police!' He pointed to a point closest to the

23 **to yell** to scream

island. 'Head for that shore! From there we'll go on by foot. If we stayed in the raft they'd catch up to us. We'd be sitting ducks!'

Tim turned to the others. 'You heard what my father said. Come on! Full speed ahead!'

While the boys paddled, Mr. Nolan tried to call the police. After a while, he shook his head. 'I can't get through. My cell signal is too weak.'

'Have you got enough signal for a text message?' Tim said.

'I don't know. I'll try it.' He typed out a message. It took several minutes. He had to say what happened, when it happened and where it happened. And he had to get it all exactly right. When he finished, he pressed the send button.

Tim gave him a worried look. 'Did it go through?'

'I'm not sure. There's no confirmation. I'll try again in a few minutes.'

As soon as they reached the opposite shore, they jumped off the raft and headed straight for the woods. When they got there, they stopped and looked back at the island. No one spoke but they were all thinking the same thought: *Where are the men who were after Len?*

Suddenly, as if in answer to their question, two men appeared on the opposite shore. When they saw the raft, they hurried down to the water's edge and looked across to where Mr. Nolan and the boys were hiding.

'We know you're there!' one of them shouted. 'Come on out! We won't harm you! We just want to talk to you!'

Tim looked at the others and put his finger on his lips. 'Quiet!' he whispered.

The two men were standing there, waiting for an answer. But not for long. A moment later, the other man shouted, 'You don't want to come out? Okay, we'll do it the hard way. You've got

2 **to be sitting ducks** to be an easy target – 13 **to go through** (*here*) to be sent (a message) – 17 **to head for** to go in the direction of – 24 **to hide** to be in a place where nobody can see you – 28 **to whisper** to speak quietly

ten seconds. If you don't come out by then, we're going to come after you!' He began counting, slowly at first, then faster. As soon as he said 'ten', the two of them jumped into the lake and started swimming towards the raft. They were strong swimmers. Shocked, Mr. Nolan and the boys watched as they moved quickly through the water.

All at once, Tim let out a loud cry and started running, the others right behind him.

Think about it ...

Did Len do the right thing by taking pictures of the men stealing the objects from the graves? Why?

Chapter 13

'Come on!' Tim shouted. 'The path is just up ahead!'

His father, Carter and Pete followed him quickly. Len kept looking back over his shoulder.

'The first camps are not far from here. We've just got to stay on the path,' Carter said.

'And hope that someone is at home!' Tim added.

They ran on. Without stopping, Mr. Nolan dialed the police again. Again there was no connection. 'I still can't get through! We've got to keep going!' he shouted.

Suddenly, Len stepped on a stone and fell. 'My ankle! I twisted my ankle!' he cried. His face was full of pain.

Immediately, everybody stopped. Tim took his hand and helped him to his feet. 'Can you walk on it?' he said.

21 **to follow** to be behind sb – 26 **to dial** to call sb

Len took in a deep breath. 'I don't think so but I'll try.' He took a step and almost fell.

Pete gave him an angry look. 'Damn it, man! Pull yourself together! They're right behind us, you know!'

'Shut up, Pete! Can't you see he's in pain?' Tim said. 'It's all right,' he said to Len. 'You're going to be all right! Put your arm around my shoulder.'

Len nodded and did what he said.

Tim turned to Pete and looked him in the eye. 'Come on, man. I need a hand,' he said.

Pete blinked with surprise. He started to shake his head but stopped suddenly. He looked at Tim and then at Len. For a moment, he just stood there, unable to decide what to do. Finally, he stepped up close to Len and let him put his arm around his shoulder. With the help of Tim and Pete, Len was able to move along slowly.

They hadn't gone far when Carter suddenly called out, 'It's a camp! I can see a camp through the trees.' He ran ahead and knocked on the door. 'Anybody there?' he shouted. He waited several seconds, then walked around to the back.

When he appeared again, he shook his head slowly. 'There's no one at home. We've got to go on.'

'You run on ahead,' said Mr. Nolan. 'We'll follow as fast as we can.' He looked back at the path and put a hand to his ear. 'We've got to hurry. They can't be far behind!'

'Why don't we trade places?' Carter said to Tim. 'You're a better runner than me. I'll help Len and you do the running.'

Tim took a quick look at Len. 'Is that okay?'

Len forced a smile. 'Don't worry about me. Get moving, man!'

Tim raced off down the path. The others watched him a moment, and then continued walking.

---

3 **to pull yourself together** to control your emotions – 10 **to need a hand** to need help – 11 **to blink** to open and close your eyes quickly – 23 **to run on** to continue running – 26 **to trade places** to exchange places – 30 **to race off** to run quickly

After a while, Len shook his head. 'Damn it!' he said. 'I'm slowing us down! They're catching up to us because of me. I should have been more careful.'

'It's not your fault, man. It could have happened to any of us,' Carter said. 'Can you keep going? How's your ankle?'

'I don't know. I can't feel it,' said Len with a little laugh. 26

'Can I have a quick look?' Len nodded and Carter bent down and pulled down Len's sock. His ankle was black and blue and all puffed up. Carter faked a smile. 'It doesn't look too bad,' he said. 'You'll be alright.'

For the next several minutes, they went on in silence. After a while, Mr. Nolan noticed that Pete seemed tired. 'Want me to take your place?' he asked.

Pete smiled. 'Thanks but not now. Maybe when Tim comes back, okay?'

'Hopefully soon,' Mr. Nolan said softly.

'With some good news for us!' Carter added.

Think about it ...

Len twisted his ankle. Have you ever twisted your ankle?

What should he do to stop the pain being too bad?

---

2 **to slow sb down** to make sb go more slowly than normal – 2 **to catch up to sb** to be able to reach sb by going more quickly than them – 9 **to fake** to pretend, to do sth that you don't really feel

Chapter 14

'Here he comes!' cried Mr. Nolan a short time later. Tim had just come around a corner in the path and was running toward them. As soon as he reached them, he gave them a thumbs down. 'I was at four or five camps,' he said. 'It was all the same. They're all locked up!'

'Oh no! That was our last chance to get help,' Carter groaned. 'The men will be here any moment now!'

Tim looked at Len. Pain was written all over his face. 'Can you hang on a little longer?' he said.

---

28 **to lock up** to close – 29 **to groan** to show your disappointment when you speak

Len forced a smile. 'I'll be all right,' he said softly.

'I'm going to try to call the police again.' Mr. Nolan took out his phone and dialed the number.

Tim and the others watched him. After a while, he shook his head. 'It's always the same: signal weak, no connection!' he said in an angry voice.

For a moment no one spoke. Finally, Tim looked around and said, 'Hey! We're not just going to stand here and wait for them to catch up, are we? Come on! We've got to keep going!'

'Wait a minute!' Len cried. He was looking across to the other end of the lake. A car had just pulled in to the public landing. Two men got out and were walking towards the boats. 'Do you see what I see?'

'Could that be the police?' Pete said.

'Dunno. It's too far away to tell,' said Tim. 'Whoever it is, we've got to do something to attract their attention.'

'Build a fire?' Carter said.

'Yeah,' said Tim. 'We've got to be quick. Come on! Let's get some dry wood as fast as we can.'

'You guys go ahead,' his father said. 'I'll stay here with Len.'

He helped Len sit down on a rock as the three boys went off into the woods. When he saw the worried look in Len's eyes, he put his hand on the boy's shoulder and tried to calm him down. But with each passing minute, Len grew more and more nervous and kept looking down the path.

Suddenly, he let out a cry. Mr. Nolan looked around and his mouth fell open. It was the two men!

When Tim and the others came out of the woods a few moments later, they got a shock! The men who had been following them were standing next to Len and his father. One of them, a small, dark-haired man with cold black eyes, had a long knife in his hand!

---

11 **to pull in** when a car pulls in, it stops

'Come on over here!' he shouted and waved his knife at them. 'And be quick about it!'

The boys looked at each other. They hesitated a moment, but then did what the man said.

He looked the four boys up and down. 'That's him!' he said finally, his eyes on Len. 'He's the one who was spying on us.' He grabbed Len by the arm and pulled. 'Come with me! We've got to have a talk.'

Len tried to hold back. 'I can't walk. I - I twisted my ankle,' he said.

The man grinned and pulled harder. 'Stop! Please!' Len cried out.

'Let go of him! Can't you see he's in pain?' Mr. Nolan shouted.

The man let out a dry laugh. 'Okay. We'll have our talk right here.' He turned to the big man beside him and pointed at the path. 'Take the others over there! Me and my little friend here want to be alone.'

The big man looked at Mr.Nolan and the others. 'You heard what he said! Come with me!'

No one moved. They were looking at Len.

The big man waited a moment, and then pulled out a knife. 'For the last time - come with me!'

'Do what he says!' Mr. Nolan said.

The three boys gave Len one more look before they turned and followed the big man. When he reached the path, he stopped and said, 'We'll wait right here.' He looked first at Mr. Nolan, then at the three boys. 'And don't any of you try to play the hero or - ' he grinned as he ran his finger along the blade of the knife - 'something bad might happen!'

Tim studied the scene below. Len was sitting on a rock. The man was standing over him with his knife pointed at Len's neck. He was shouting. *Please don't hurt him,* Tim thought to himself and felt his heart slow down until it seemed to stop.

---

6 **to spy on sb** to watch what sb is doing without being noticed – 12 **to let go of sb** to stop holding onto sb – 27 **blade** the sharp part of a knife

'While we're waiting,' said the big man in a cold voice, 'I want all of you to give me your phones.' He held out his hand.

Mr. Nolan, Carter and Pete handed over their phones immediately. Tim shook his head.

'I'm warning you!' the man hissed. He pointed his knife at Tim and took a step forward.

'Tim! Please! Give him your phone!' his father cried.

Think about it ...

How do you think the boys will escape?

If you were in this situation, would you give the men your mobile phone?

3 **to hand over** to give sth to sb

Chapter 15

'STAY WHERE YOU ARE! THIS IS THE POLICE!' The loud voice boomed over the water. Everyone stopped and looked around. A large white boat was speeding across the lake toward them. Tim could see two men in it. One of them had a bullhorn and was standing at the front. The other was looking towards them through binoculars.

The small man reacted immediately. 'Let's get out of here!' he shouted to the other man. They turned and ran for the woods. Tim tried to take photos of them with his phone, but they were too far away already.

For a moment, everyone had forgotten about Len, but now they hurried over to him and helped him up. 'Are you all right?' Tim asked.

Len let out a deep breath and nodded slowly.

'Did he get your Smartphone?' Carter said.

20 **to be speeding** to be going fast – 21 **bullhorn** loud speaker – 23 **binoculars** sth you can use to see things that are far away

'He tried to,' Len said with a grin. 'But he didn't think to look here!' He pointed to the hood of his sweatshirt and let out a nervous laugh.

Pete gave Len an admiring look. 'Cool move, man,' he said.

The others laughed and patted Len on the back.

A moment later, the sound of the boat made them turn. It was close now and moving quickly toward them. They could see the two men clearly now. They were police officers. Moments later, they reached shore and got out of the boat.

'Hello! I'm Officer Riley,' the taller one said. He nodded at the man beside him. 'And this is Officer Pickett. We got your text message and came at once. We phoned the warden and he let us use his boat.'

'You got here just in time!' said Mr. Nolan.

Officer Riley smiled at him. 'Can you tell us what this is all about? Take your time. Start from the beginning.'

Mr. Nolan hesitated. 'It's a long story,' he said and looked at Tim. 'I think my son can tell it better than I can.'

'Yeah, well, it all started with me,' Tim explained. 'It was my idea to build a raft with my friends and raft down the lake to Indian Island. My dad agreed to come with us.'

Officer Riley listened carefully while Officer Pickett took notes. 'Go on, please,' said Officer Riley.

'When we reached the island, we decided to go and see the Indian burial ground.' Tim pointed at Len. 'When we got there, Len felt sick and went off by himself. Then a man with a rifle came along and asked us what we were doing on the island. We told him that we wanted to have a look at the burial ground and he offered to show us around. He said it was his job to guard it.' Tim paused and let out a little laugh.

'What's so funny?' Officer Riley wanted to know.

2 **hood** the part of a sweatshirt or jacket you can pull over your head – 12 **warden** sb in charge of a building

'We found his story hard to believe,' Tim said. Again he paused. 'Yeah, and while he was showing us around, Len - he was on the top of a little hill - noticed two men on the other side of the burial ground. They were digging up graves! He got up closer to take photos of them, but' – he paused and nodded at Len – 'I think Len can best tell you what happened after that.'

'But they saw me and started chasing me,' Len said in a shaky voice. 'I warned the others and all of us ran to the raft. Then we paddled as hard as we could to the opposite shore and hid. The two men weren't far behind. When they saw our raft, they shouted to us and said they wanted to talk to us.' He paused and took in a deep breath. It was hard for him to talk about what had happened. 'We didn't move. We were very frightened.'

'But when they jumped in the water and started swimming towards us, we ran for our lives!' Mr. Nolan said. 'We hoped to reach a camp and get some help.'

'But then I fell and twisted my ankle and that slowed us down.' Len frowned and lowered his eyes.

'What happened after that?' Officer Riley turned to Mr. Nolan again.

Suddenly, Tim shook his head. 'I don't mean to be disrespectful, Officer Riley, but while we're standing around here talking, the two men are getting away!'

Officer Riley smiled at him. 'Don't worry about that. I've already put out an alert on them. Right now it's important for me to get the facts. That's what we're doing here. So let's just continue if you don't mind.' He turned back to Tim's father.

'Sure. Well, after Len twisted his ankle, Carter, Pete and I stayed with him while Tim ran on ahead to see if he could get help,' he said. 'He went to several camps but they were all locked up. Yeah, and when - ' Tim cut in, 'When I returned from the camps - that's when we caught sight of you across the lake at the public landing.'

'We were gathering wood to build an S.O.S. fire when the grave diggers caught up with us,' Carter added quickly. 'One of them grabbed Len and began to search him. He was looking for his phone - for the photos Len took of them.'

Len grinned from ear to ear. 'But he didn't find it! I hid it here!' He pointed at the hood of his sweatshirt.

Pete let out a loud laugh. 'And then we heard that big, beautiful voice say STAY WHERE YOU ARE, THIS IS THE POLICE!'

'The men heard it, too, and ran for the woods. I tried to take photos of them but they were already quite far away with their backs to the camera. The photos aren't much good,' said Tim.

'But mine are!' Len said and gave Officer Riley the thumbs up sign. 'The ones of them digging up the graves!'

1 **grave digger** sb whose job it is to dig graves

Officer Riley smiled. 'Would you let us use those photos to help identify the men?'

'I'd be happy to, Officer,' Len said with a grin.

Officer Riley looked at Mr. Nolan and the boys. 'Well, I guess that's it. Thank you very much. You've been a big help to us.' Suddenly he smiled and said, 'Perhaps we can do something for you. You must be tired and hungry. Why don't you get in the boat with us and we'll take you back to where you put the raft in?'

Mr. Nolan nodded quickly and looked at the boys. 'We'll be happy to. Right, guys?'

'But Dad, what about the raft?'

'We can come and get it later, okay? Besides, we've got to get Len to a doctor as soon as possible.'

Officer Riley nodded and said, 'You can give Officer Pickett your names and addresses when we get in the boat.'

'Our names won't be in the media, will they?' Mr. Nolan asked.

Officer Riley thought for a moment, and then shook her head. 'No, they won't. I'll see to it that your names stay out of the media. That's a promise.'

Mr. Nolan nodded. 'Thanks, Officer!' he said in a loud voice.

'Okay. All aboard! Let's get going!' Officer Riley waited until everyone was in the boat and then started the motor.

As they speeded across the lake, Mr. Nolan looked around at the boys. They were strangely quiet, each of them busy with their own thoughts.

Think about it ...

- Why do you think the boys are quiet?
- How do you think the police will catch the men?

2 **to identify** to be able to tell who sb is

Chapter 16

Two days later the boys met at the clubhouse again. Len arrived last. There was tape around his ankle and he was limping. When they went inside and everyone was sitting around the table, Tim opened his backpack and pulled out a six-pack of sparkling water and a large bag.

'Something to eat?' Pete said.

Tim smiled. 'Yep, something to eat.'

Pete's eyes opened wide. 'For us?'

'Sure. From my father. It's his way of saying thanks,' Tim said.

'For what?' Len wanted to know.

'For like, you know, going with us on the raft. He said it was an experience he'll never forget!' Tim let out a little laugh, then opened the bag. Pete's eyes almost popped out. It was full of jelly donuts! 'So, come on, help yourselves!'

While the boys were eating, Tim took out his phone, clicked on an app and began to read something. 'Hey! he said a moment later. 'Listen to this! It's from today's Bangor Daily News!'

GRAVE ROBBERS ON INDIAN ISLAND

At a press conference Thursday afternoon, Madawaska Police Chief Larry Leblanc talked about grave robbers at the Indian burial ground on Indian Island. He said that after receiving an anonymous tip, the police acted quickly and arrested two men found there, and put out an alert for two other men. After an intensive search, including the use of a helicopter, the men were caught early Thursday morning just as they were about to cross the border near Grand Isle into Canada. According to Police Chief Leblanc, this was the first case of grave robbery on Indian Island. He described the operation as the work of professionals, part of a well-organized gang. There is a huge black market for the pots, masks and jewelry taken from Indian graves, he

2 **to limp** to have problems walking due to an injury – 20 **Police Chief** the most important police officer – 23 **to arrest sb** to make sb come with them to the police station to ask them questions – 30 **gang** a criminal organization – 30 **black market** market where illegal things are sold

explained. Chief Leblanc said he could understand the terrible shock to the Maliseet community caused by this awful crime and promised to do all he could to help recover the stolen goods. He closed the conference by praising his officers for their good work.

When Tim finished reading, he looked around into the faces of the others and smiled.

Len jumped up and let out a loud laugh. 'They got them! They got them!' he said again and again.

'Yep, they got the little fish. Hopefully, they'll get the big fish, too,' said Carter.

'They will,' Len said. 'It's just a matter of time.'

'And Officer Riley kept his word,' said Carter to Tim. 'Just like your dad wanted.'

Pete frowned and wiped some jelly from around his mouth. 'Huh? Kept his word? What do you mean?'

Carter looked up from his Smartphone and laughed. 'The police didn't use our names! They said they got an "anonymous tip".'

'Uh, what's that?'

'Anonymous means somebody, anybody. The tip came from 'somebody', get it?'

Pete looked puzzled. 'Somebody? Yeah, but from who?'

Carter rolled his eyes. 'Duh! From somebody! It means it could be anybody! It means the police don't know who the tip came from!'

'But they know we gave them the tip, don't they?' Pete protested.

'Sure they know. But they're not saying who because they promised to keep our names out of the newspapers.'

Pete still didn't get it, but he laughed, as if he had understood.

After that, they goofed around for a while, but it wasn't long before they began talking about what had happened on the lake. They *had* to talk about it. It was like an awesome movie, a *very* awesome movie, and they were the stars of that movie. They

18 **tip** important information needed to solve a case – 29 **to goof around** to behave in a silly way – 31 **awesome** incredible

talked in loud, excited voices and laughed a lot. But after a while, Tim suddenly grew quiet. There was a troubled look on his face.

'Sometimes I wonder what would have happened if - ' he began, then paused to find the right words to say what he was thinking.

'If what?' Pete cut in.

Carter shook his head at Pete. 'Tim means what would have happened if things had gone differently. If, like, the police hadn't got his father's text message.'

'Oh, okay. We were lucky, weren't we?' Pete said. 'Of course, we wouldn't have gotten into so much trouble if Len hadn't taken photos of the grave robbers,' he added and gave Len a playful smile.

Len thought about that for a moment and then said in a calm voice, 'I'm sorry for the trouble I caused, but I'm happy that we helped stop the grave robbers. I'm not sure I believe everything my grandmother told me about Indian burial grounds, but I do think she was right when she said that we should let the dead rest in peace.'

'Me, too,' said Tim quickly and put his hand on Len's shoulder. Then, for a moment, he said nothing. He seemed to be lost in thought. When he finally spoke, his words came out slowly. 'You know, basically I'm the one who got us in trouble. It was my idea to raft to the island.' He lowered his eyes and looked at his hands. 'When I think about what might have happened, I feel really bad. It was a stupid idea! It could have got us killed!'

'Come on, man, you're being too hard on yourself,' Carter said. 'We wanted to go with you. Remember? You didn't force us to go, did you?'

Tim smiled weakly and nodded.

'Besides, how could you know about the grave robbers?'

---

21 **to be lost in thought** to be thinking deeply – 27 **to be too hard on yourself** to blame yourself unfairly for sth

Tim thought about that a moment. 'You're right, I couldn't,' he said at last. Suddenly, he smiled. He looked around at the others. 'Apart from the fact that we helped the police stop the grave robbers, the whole thing was - ' he paused to take a deep breath - 'it was, uh, an adventure, an unbelievable experience, one I'll remember for a long time, I'm sure of that!'

For a long moment, no one spoke. They were all looking at Tim. At last Carter turned to the others. His eyes were shining. 'Tim's right,' he said. 'It was an adventure! A great big fat adventure! One that none of us will forget! Not ever!' Suddenly he stood up, smiled and gave each of the boys a happy high five.

Tim, Len and Pete were so surprised at first that they just stared at Carter. They had never known him to get so excited. After a while, they started nodding. Finally, Pete said in a loud voice, 'Right on, man!' and they all began to laugh, softly at first, then louder and louder, Tim loudest of all.

Think about it ...

Why do you think the boys didn't want to be in the media?

How would you feel about this?

Activities

Focus on the story

1. Are these sentences True or False?

Tick the correct box.

		True	False
1.	The clubhouse was near a lake.	☐	☐
2.	Pete had the idea about building a draft.	☐	☐
3.	Carter wasn't very excited about building a raft.	☐	☐
4.	Tim's father went on the raft with the boys.	☐	☐
5.	Pete is of Indian heritage.	☐	☐
6.	It took them more than a week to build the raft.	☐	☐
7.	It was safe to swim at the lake.	☐	☐
8.	Len was a good rapper.	☐	☐
9.	They decided to stay near the shore because it was safer.	☐	☐
10.	They used pages from a comic book to make a fire.	☐	☐
11.	Johnny worked as a guard because he liked to be in the woods.	☐	☐
12.	The men were stealing expensive pots from the graves.	☐	☐
13.	A pot could cost up to $10,000.	☐	☐
14.	The men gave the boys a long tour of the burial site.	☐	☐
15.	Len took photos of the men stealing things from the graves.	☐	☐
16.	Pete twisted his ankle when they were running away from the thieves.	☐	☐
17.	Mr. Nolan managed to get a signal to call the police.	☐	☐
18.	The thieves managed to run away from the police.	☐	☐
19.	The boys wanted to be in the newspapers.	☐	☐
20.	The boys were very happy about the adventure they experienced.	☐	☐

2. What happened when?

Put the events in the correct order. Write the number in the correct box below.

a The boys agreed not to use their smartphones on the raft.
b. They found the Indian burial ground.
c. Len turned a sea shanty into a rap.
d. Tim had the idea to build a raft when he saw the fallen trees.
e. Carter checked how to build a raft.
f. There was a big storm, and a lot of trees fell.
g. The boys finished building their clubhouse.
h. Len took photos of the thieves.
i. The boys had doughnuts in the clubhouse.
j. The boys celebrated their adventure.

a	b	c	d	e	f	g	h	i	j
						1			

3. Where did they come in the story?

Put the following places in the order they were mentioned in the book.

the police boat
Indian Island
the cove
the camp sites
the lake
the clubhouse
the burial grounds

1	2	3	4	5	6	7

4. What happened where?

Match the place with the event that happened there.

1 the clubhouse	a. the place where they couldn't find anyone who could help them escape
2 Indian island	b. the place where the guards worked
3 the burial grounds	c. the place Len didn't want to go to
4 the camp site	d. the place that the boys built and where the boys meet
5 the hut	e. the place that the boys wanted to explore

Focus on the people

1. Were you right?

Match the character from the story with what happened.

a. Len	b. Carter	c. Tim	d. Mr. Nolan	d. Pete

1. ____________ had the idea to build a raft.
2. ____________ had to go and get pizzas and soft drinks when they had finished building the clubhouse.
3. ____________ was in charge of building the raft.
4. ____________ had a bad dream the night before going on the raft.
5. ____________ had Indian relatives.
6. ____________ was good at rapping.
7. ____________ gave a page from his comic to build a fire.
8. ____________ twisted his ankle.
9. ____________ texted the police and asked for help.
10. ____________ bought doughnuts to celebrate the adventure they had.

2. What do you know about Len?

Write Len's profile, and then your profile.

Name: Len		Me:	
Heritage: **Favourite type of music:** **Biggest fear:**		**Heritage:** **Favourite type of music:** **Biggest fear:**	

Focus on grammar

1. What's the question?

Write the questions for the following answers.

1 Where ______________________________________?
The clubhouse was near a lake.

2. Why ______________________________________ as a guard?
Johnny worked as a guard because he liked to be in the woods.

3. When ________________________________ at the clubhouse?
They met at the clubhouse the next morning at nine o'clock.

4. Where ______________________________ the paddles?
Tim hid the paddles in the clubhouse.

5. Why ______________________________ a page of his comic book?
Pete gave Tim a page of his comic book so that he could start a fire.

6. Who ______________________________?
Tim tried to take photos of the men.

2. Which preposition fits?

Choose the correct preposition in each sentence.

1. We all know how good you are at / in / with rapping!
2. The boys know nothing over / about / on how to build a raft.
3. Len's grandma taught him on / about / over Indian burial grounds.
4. Len is worried at / about / over going to Indian Island.
5. Come on, guys, let's get in / into / through the water.
6. There was fog over / above / on the lake.

Build your vocabulary

Focus on words

1. What's the expression?

Find the word in the puzzle and check that you know what it means. Use the words to talk about what happened in the story.

clubhouse	lake	raft	island	log	fog	storm	police
guards	binoculars	diggers					

U	V	L	C	Q	F	O	G	B	X
Q	P	O	L	I	C	E	D	I	N
G	W	G	U	I	Q	O	I	N	W
U	O	R	B	Y	M	M	G	O	S
A	J	A	H	R	L	H	G	C	F
R	J	F	O	L	A	K	E	U	J
D	M	T	U	R	I	P	R	L	B
S	S	O	S	Y	H	G	S	A	P
M	T	Y	E	X	D	S	G	R	Z
P	D	I	S	L	A	N	D	S	S

2. Phrasal verbs

Fill in the gaps with a phrasal verb from the box.

~~let out~~	put out	get out	look out	find out	hold out

Example: Len was nervous so he let **out** a nervous laugh,

1 The guards were ___________ for intruders.
2 The boys ___________ that the thieves were stealing from the graves.
3 One of the thieves asked the boys for their phone, and then ___________ his hand.
4 The boys managed to ___________ of the dangerous area of the lake just in time.
5 When their clothes were dry, they carefully ________ the fire.

Buried Treasure on Indian Island – the mind map

You can add any words from the glossary to this mind map for your own learning.

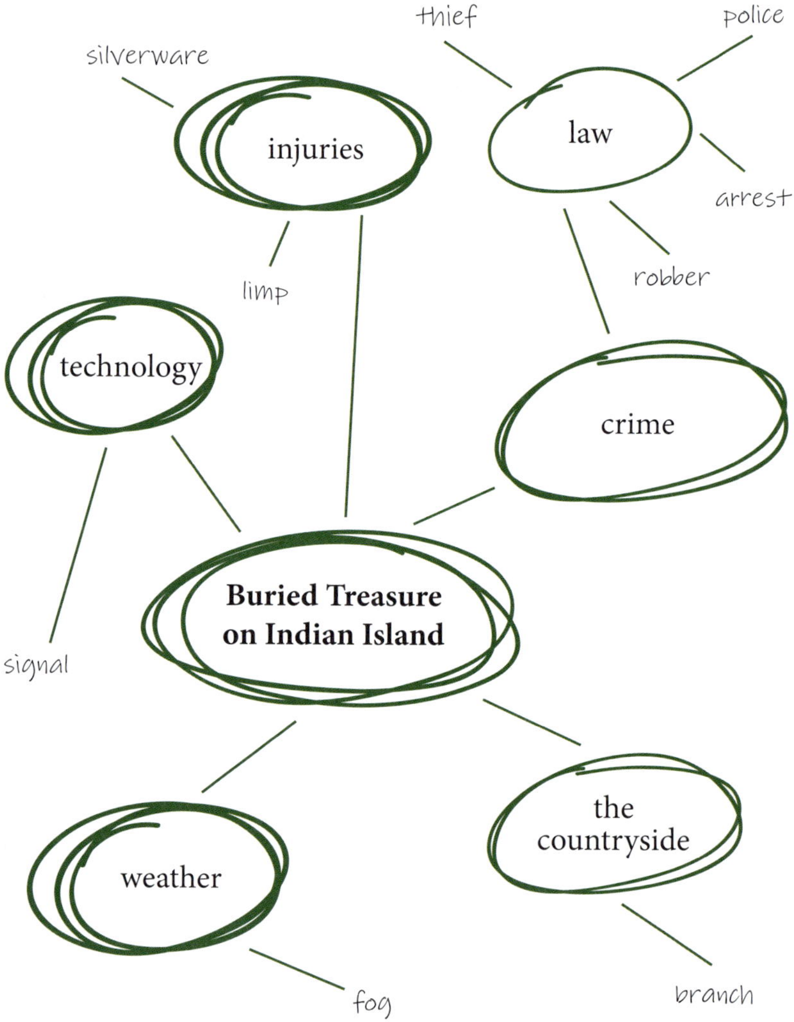

Glossary

	New word?	Notes / connected words
Crime		
arrest	☐	
be caught	☐	
black market	☐	
gang	☐	
grave digger	☐	
intensive search	☐	
run away	☐	
police	☐	
police helicopter	☐	
robber	☐	
stolen goods	☐	
thief	☐	
Injuries		
bruised	☐	
limp	☐	
poke your eye	☐	
puffed up	☐	
run into something	☐	
see a doctor	☐	
twist your ankle	☐	
Technology		
camera	☐	
online	☐	
photos	☐	
signal	☐	
smartphone	☐	
text message	☐	

	New word?	Notes / connected words
Weather		
cool breeze	☐	
fog	☐	
long and cold winter	☐	
rough conditions	☐	
storm	☐	
strong wind	☐	
sunny	☐	
warm	☐	
The countryside		
board	☐	
branches	☐	
hill	☐	
leaves	☐	
log	☐	
shore	☐	
step on a snake	☐	
thick and dark forest	☐	

Find out more

1. How to build a raft

You and your friends want to build a raft. Search online and write the instructions for building a raft in 10 steps.

1
2
3
4
5
6
7
8
9
10

2. Native Americans

1. Since the arrival of European explorers on the American continent, the lives of Native Americans have changed a lot.

Find out about how Native Americans live now. Put the information you find in the table below.

Situation	Facts	Reason
money		
school and higher education		
addiction		
mental and physical health		
crime		

2. In March 2021 Deb Haaland became the first Native American to become the U.S. Secretary of the Interior. If you were Deb Haaland, what would you want to change and how would you change it?

Make a poster to present your ideas.

Answer key

Focus on the story

1.

1. T, 2. F, 3. T, 4. T, 5. T, 6. F, 7. F, 8. T, 9. T, 10. T, 11. F, 12. T, 13. F, 14. F, 15. T, 16. F, 17. F, 18. F, 19. T, 20. T

2.

a	b	c	d	e	f	g	h	i	j
5	7	6	3	4	2	1	8	9	10

3.

1	2	3	4	5	6	7
the clubhouse	the lake	Indian Island	the burial grounds	the cove	the camp sites	the police boat

4. 1. d, 2. e, 3. C, 4. a, 5. b

Focus on the people

1. 1. C, 2. B, 3. C, 4. A, 5. A, 6. A, 7. A, 8. D, 9. D
2. Len: Indian, Rap, Indian burial grounds

Focus on grammar

1. 1. Where was the clubhouse? 2. Why did Johnny work as a guard? 3. When and where did they meet the next morning? 4. Where did Tim hide the paddles? 5. Why did Pete give Tim a page of his comic book? 6. Who tried to take photos of the men?
2. 1. at, 2. about, 3. about, 4. about, 5. Into, 6. on

Focus on vocabulary

1.

U	V	L	C	Q	F	O	G	B	X
Q	P	O	L	I	C	E	D	I	N
G	W	G	U	I	Q	O	I	N	W
U	O	R	B	Y	M	M	G	O	S
A	J	A	H	R	L	H	G	C	F
R	J	F	O	L	A	K	E	U	J
D	M	T	U	R	I	P	R	L	B
S	S	O	S	Y	H	G	S	A	P
M	T	Y	E	X	D	S	G	R	Z
P	D	I	S	L	A	N	D	S	S

2.

1. looking out, 2. found out, 3. held out, 4. get out, 5. put out